NOTE TO PARENTS

Although every magic trick in this book has been kid-tested, and can, with practice, be easily performed by most children, some tricks are more difficult than others and may require your supervision. Please read every trick before allowing your child to do it. The RGA Publishing Group and SMITHMARK Publishers will not be held responsible for any injury that occurs during the practice or performance of a trick.

An RGA Book

ISBN 0-8317-6239-X

Hoppin' Magic

My First
Cup, Ball, & Paper
MAGIC
TRICKS

Written by Stephanie Johnson

Illustrated by Kerry Manwaring

SMITHMARK

Unpoppable!

In this trick, a pin is inserted into an ordinary balloon without popping it!

What You'll Need:
- A balloon
- A pin or needle
- Transparent tape

Getting Ready:

1. Blow up the balloon.

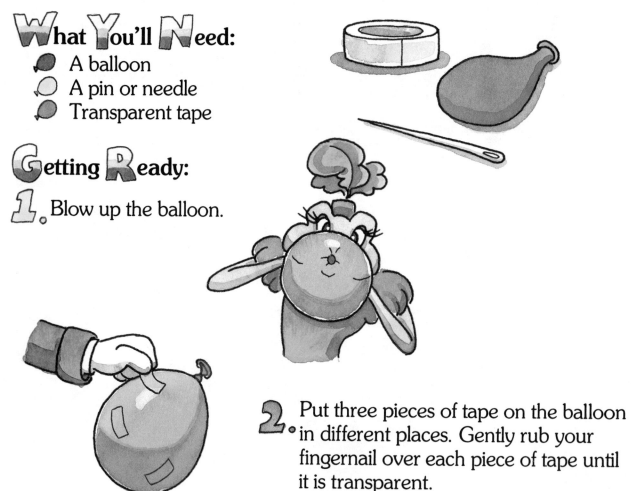

2. Put three pieces of tape on the balloon in different places. Gently rub your fingernail over each piece of tape until it is transparent.

Doing the Trick:

1. Start by holding the balloon up in front of your audience and saying, "This is a magic unpoppable balloon."

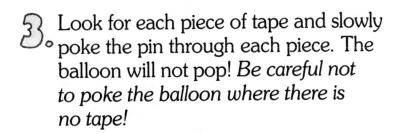

2. Pick up the pin or needle in one hand and say, "I will now demonstrate that this balloon is unpoppable."

3. Look for each piece of tape and slowly poke the pin through each piece. The balloon will not pop! *Be careful not to poke the balloon where there is no tape!*

What's in a Name?

With this trick, you can pretend to hypnotize someone into obeying your command!

What You'll Need:

- A shoe box with a lid
- Pencils
- A piece of thin cardboard as long and as wide as the box
- Several pieces of paper, all the same size

Getting Ready:

1. Take the lid off the shoe box. Cut the cardboard so that it fits perfectly into the lid, *but not so snugly that it won't drop out easily.*

2. Write your name on as many pieces of the paper as there are members of your audience. Fold each of these papers in half, then put them into the lid of the shoe box and spread them out evenly. Then put the cardboard into the lid to cover the papers.

Doing the Trick:

1. Hand out a pencil and a piece of paper to each member of your audience. Ask everyone to write down their names. Tell them you are writing your name on a piece of paper, too, then do so.

2. Now ask everyone to fold their papers once, then drop it into the shoe box. Drop the paper with your name into the box, too.

3. Set the box on your show table. Use your hand to spread the names evenly across the bottom of the box.

4. Pick up the lid, holding the cardboard piece tightly with your fingers to keep it from falling out. Carefully put the lid on the box. Unseen by your audience, the cardboard piece will drop down and cover all the names that were dropped into the box. The pieces of paper that have *your* name written on them will be on top of the piece of cardboard at the bottom of the box.

5. Tap the top of the box with your magic wand and say some magic words. Tell your audience, "I will now magically hypnotize someone to draw a certain name from my magic box."

6. Ask for a volunteer. Wave your wand over his or her head and say, "You will now draw my name from the box."

Mr. Magic Rabbit

7. Take the lid off the box and hold the box high in the air. Have the volunteer draw out a piece of paper and read it to the audience. It will be your name!

News with a Bounce

Turn an ordinary newspaper into a bouncing ball. How?
It's hoppin' magic!

What You'll Need:

- ⚪ A small, hard rubber ball
- ⚫ A sheet of newspaper
- 🔵 Masking tape

Getting Ready:

1. Tape the ball to one corner of the newspaper. Be sure that it cannot be seen from the other side of the paper.

2. Fold up the newspaper and put it in your pocket or under your show table.

Doing the Trick:

1. First take out the newspaper and unfold it in front of your audience. Keep your hand over the corner with the ball so that the audience does not see it.

2. Hold up the newspaper by the corners. Say, "I will now turn this newspaper into a bouncing ball."

3. Crumple up the newspaper around the ball so that the ball is hidden in the paper.

4. Set the crumpled paper on the table and say, "See, I've turned it into a ball."

5. Your audience will groan and think it is a stupid trick—that is, until you pick up the newspaper and throw it on the floor. Everyone will be surprised to see it bounce!

True Colors

Change a red ball into a blue ball in a few simple steps!

What You'll Need:

- A small piece of red construction paper and a small piece of blue construction paper, both the same size
- 2 Styrofoam cups
- Scissors

Getting Ready:

1. Crumple up each piece of construction paper into a small ball.

2. Cut the bottom off one of the cups.

3. Put the blue ball into the other cup.

Doing the Trick:

1. Set the two cups and the red ball on your show table. *Do not let your audience see the hole in the bottom of the one cup or the blue ball in the other cup.*

2. Now pick up the bottomless cup with your left hand and set it in the palm of your right hand. Again, *be careful not to let anyone see that the bottom is missing.*

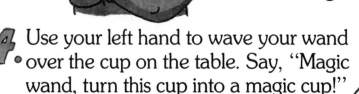

3. Pick up the red ball and say, "I'm going to change the color of this red ball." Put it into the cup in your right hand.

4. Use your left hand to wave your wand over the cup on the table. Say, "Magic wand, turn this cup into a magic cup!"

5. Put down your wand. Use your left hand to take the cup from your right hand. The red ball will stay in your right hand. Close your hand quickly to hide the red ball.

6. Quickly drop the ball into your pocket or onto the floor so no one will see it. As you do this, slide the bottomless cup into the other cup on the table.

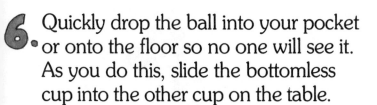

7. Ask the audience, "What color is the ball in the cup?" They will answer, "Red."

8. Turn over the double cup. The blue ball will roll out!

Mind Over Crayon

With this trick, you can use "mind power" to guess the color of a crayon without looking at it!

What You'll Need:
⭐ A box of crayons

Doing the Trick:

1. Ask for a volunteer from the audience. Give the volunteer the box of crayons. Say, "I will identify the color of any crayon you choose without looking at the crayon."

2. Turn your back to the volunteer and the audience. Put your hands together behind you.

3. Ask the volunteer to hand you a crayon. Then, *without letting anyone see you do it,* take the crayon and quickly scrape the thumbnail of your left hand on the crayon wax. Then turn and face the audience.

4. Keep the crayon behind your back with your right hand and bring your left hand to your forehead. Quickly look at the wax on your thumbnail and note the color.

5. Close your eyes for a few seconds and pretend you are thinking hard. Announce the color to your audience and ask the volunteer, "Am I right?" You will be!

Clippin' Clips

This trick is so much fun, you'll want to do it over and over to figure out how it works!

What You'll Need:

△ A strip of construction paper about 6 inches long and 1 inch wide
▲ 2 large paper clips
△ A rubber band (roughly the same size as the paper clips)

Doing the Trick:

1. Fold the strip of paper in half and loop the rubber band over one half near the crease.

2. Clip the two halves of the paper strip together in the middle.

3. Hold the paper so that the rubber band is on the outside of the side facing you. Fold the front half of the paper over the rubber band.

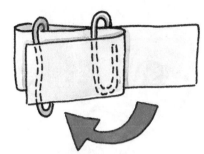

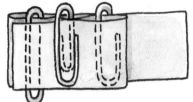

4. Fasten the second paper clip between the rubber band and the first clip, *but only over the top two layers of paper.*

5. Hold one end of the paper in your left hand and the opposite end in your right hand. Pull the ends away from each other with a fast, hard tug. The paper clips and the rubber band will magically link together! *Make sure you tug quickly, otherwise the trick won't work.*

Mind Magic

THIS TRICK IS A GREAT ONE TO FOOL YOUR YOUNGER BROTHER OR SISTER!

You can use your mind power to make a person do what you want. Now that's using your head!

What You'll Need:

- A book
- A key
- A piece of paper
- A cup
- A pencil

Doing the Trick:

1. Start by setting the book, cup, and key on your show table. Tell your audience, "I have here three ordinary objects. I will now write down the name of one of these objects on a piece of paper and give it to someone in the audience."

2. Write the name of one of the objects on the piece of paper. Fold it and hand it to the nearest person in the audience. Tell that person not to read what you have written or show it to anyone else.

3. Now ask for a volunteer. Tell the volunteer, "I am going to use my mind to make you show me the object I wrote down."

4. Have the volunteer pick up two of the objects on the table. If neither of these two objects is the one you wrote down, then you have completed the trick. Say, "The remaining object is the object I wrote down." Ask the person holding the paper to read out loud what you wrote.

5. If the volunteer does pick up the object that you wrote down, say, "Now give me one of the objects." If he or she hands you the object that you wrote down, hold it up and say, "This is the object I wrote down." Ask the person holding the paper to read out loud what you wrote.

6. If the volunteer hands you one of the objects and is still holding the object you wrote down, point to the volunteer and say, "You are holding the object I chose." Ask the person holding the paper to read out loud what you wrote. This is a simple process-of-elimination trick that will fool your family and friends!

The Great Balloon Blow-Up

Baffle your buddies by blowing up a balloon without even touching it!

What You'll Need:

- 2 balloons of the same size and color
- A large paper bag
- A paper clip Tape

Getting Ready:

1. Blow up one balloon half full and tie it closed. Use a small piece of tape to fasten the balloon inside the paper bag.

2. Blow up the second balloon all the way and close it off with a paper clip as shown.

3. Set the second balloon on top of the first balloon inside the bag.

Doing the Trick:

1. Show the bag to your audience, then turn it upside down over your show table. The balloon with the paper clip will fall out. The other balloon will stay taped inside the bag, unseen by your audience.

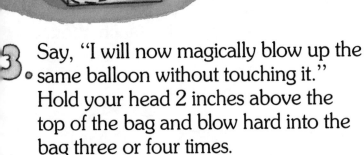

2. Set the bag on your table. Say, "I will now let the air out of this balloon." Remove the paper clip and let the air out. Drop the deflated balloon into the bag.

3. Say, "I will now magically blow up the same balloon without touching it." Hold your head 2 inches above the top of the bag and blow hard into the bag three or four times.

4. Reach into the bag. Pull out the balloon you blew up earlier, *being careful to leave the tape and the deflated balloon inside the bag!*

Loop-de-Loop

HOCUS POCUS, ZIPPIDY ZOOP! MAKE THIS RING A GIANT LOOP!

Here's a trick with a special *twist*. Follow the directions carefully, and it will come off like a charm!

What You'll Need:

- 2 sheets of newspaper
- Scissors
- Glue or rubber cement

Getting Ready:

1. Cut two long strips (each about 2 inches wide) from the newspaper.

2. Glue the ends of one strip together to form a loop.

3. Hold the ends of the other strip together to form a loop. But first, twis the loop one complete turn and then glue the ends together. *The trick wor work if you don't twist the strip first.*

Doing the Trick:

1. Lay the two loops on your show table. Tell your audience, "I have two ordinary paper loops. I will now cut one loop in half."

2. Pick up the loop that is not twisted. Use the end of the scissors to poke a hole in the paper.

3. Cut the loop in half following the dotted line as shown. When you have finished cutting, you will have two separate loops. Show the loops to the audience and lay them down on the table.

4. Hold up the loop that is twisted. Say, "What will happen when I cut this paper loop in half?" Your audience will answer, "You'll get two loops again."

5. Now proclaim, "I'm going to cast a magic spell on this paper loop before I cut it in half." Wave your wand over the loop and say, "Hocus pocus, zippidy zoop! Make this ring a giant loop!"

6. Use the scissors to poke a hole in the loop and cut it in half following the dotted line. When you have finished, your audience will be surprised to see that you have not two loops, but one GIANT loop!

Colored Cards

You'll really mystify your friends with this trick!

What You'll Need:

- Red, blue, yellow, and green construction paper
- Scissors ☐ A ruler
- A pencil
- Glue or rubber cement
- A black marker
- A large paper bag

Getting Ready:

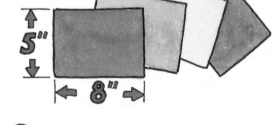

1. Using the ruler, pencil, and scissors, measure and cut out a card about 8 inches long and 5 inches wide from each piece of construction paper.

2. Using the black marker, write SORRY! on one side of the green card and WRONG AGAIN! on the other side.

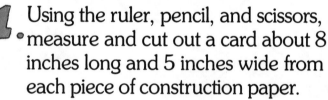

3. Paste the blue card over the red card at the angle shown in the diagram. Now you have a "double card." Trim along the outside edge of the blue card.

4. Roll down the edges of your paper bag about 3 inches and set it neatly on your table. Put the green card into the bag.

Doing the Trick:

1. Fan out the yellow and blue/red cards and show them to your audience. Be sure that the blue/red card is behind the yellow card when you do this so it appears that you are fanning out three separate cards of different colors.

2. Say, "I have three cards in my hand. One is blue, one is red, and one is yellow."

3. Then drop the cards into the paper bag with the green card. Shake the bag and wave your magic wand over it.

4. Reach into the bag and pull out the yellow card. Show it to the audience and put it down on the table.

5. Reach in again and pull out the blue/red card, *but do not show the audience the two-colored side.* Show them the backside, which is completely red. Put the card on the table, red side up.

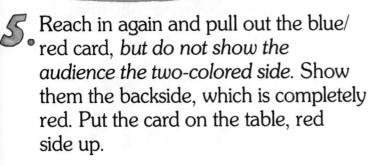

6. Ask the audience, "Which card is still in the bag?" They will say, "The blue card."

7. Reach into the bag and pull out the green card. Show the audience the side that reads, SORRY! If someone asks to see the other side, flip it over and show them the side that reads, WRONG AGAIN!

Dueling Bands

Here's a quick and simple trick to amaze your friends and family. And all you need is a couple of rubber bands!

What You'll Need:

- Two rubber bands, each of a different color

Doing the Trick:

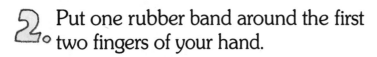

1. Hold up one rubber band. Say, "This rubber band will magically jump from one finger to the other."

2. Put one rubber band around the first two fingers of your hand.

3. Now loop the rubber band around all your fingertips just above your fingernails. Don't loop the rubber band around your thumb.

4. Open your hand quickly. The band will jump to your third and fourth fingers!

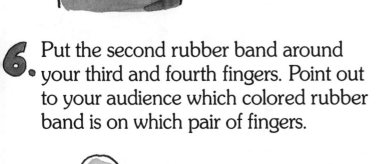

5. Say, "Now I will do the same with two rubber bands." Put one rubber band around your first and second fingers.

6. Put the second rubber band around your third and fourth fingers. Point out to your audience which colored rubber band is on which pair of fingers.

7. Loop both rubber bands around all your fingertips just above your fingernails. Again, do not loop the rubber band around your thumb.

8. Quickly open your hand. The first band will jump to your third and fourth fingers, and the second band will jump to your first and second fingers!

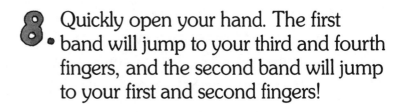

Heads Up!

Here's a trick you'll need to try many times before you perform it. But with practice, you'll soon be right "on the money"!

What You'll Need:

- ☆ A piece of thick cardboard, at least 6 inches by 6 inches
- ★ Silver or gold poster paint
- ★ Black marker   ☆ A paintbrush
- ★ A bowl, approximately 6 inches in diameter
- ☆ Scissors   ★ A pencil
- ★ White paper   ★ Glue

Getting Ready:

1. Place the bowl face down on the cardboard and trace around it with the pencil. Now cut a 6-inch-wide circle from the cardboard. This will be your magic coin. Paint the coin silver or gold. Let the paint dry overnight.

2. Draw two identical profiles of a person's head, one for each side of the coin. Here's how you can do this: On a separate piece of paper, draw a head using the black marker. Then put another piece of paper over your drawing and trace it with the marker.

3. Cut out the heads and paste one on each side of your coin in the positions shown to the right.

FRONT   BACK

4. The diagram shows three sets of points. Write these points in very small letters, so your audience can't see them. You will use these points to rotate the coin between your fingers.

Doing the Trick:

1. If you hold the coin at the places shown and turn the coin over, both heads will face to the right. Say to your audience, "I have here a magical two-headed coin." Rotate the coin on the A points to show that it has a head on each side.

2. Say, "The funny thing about this coin is that the heads just keep moving around. . . ." Hold the coin at the next two places shown and rotate it on the B points. The head will face to the right on the front of the coin and be upside down on the back!

3. Now say, "And they never seem to end up in the same place twice!" Hold the coin at the next two places shown and rotate it on the C points to make the heads move again. The head will face to the right on the front of the coin and downward on the back!